SUPERCHARGE YOUR SELLING

NIGEL HENZELL-THOMAS

Hutchinson Business

SUPERCHARGE YOUR SELLING

I don't know who you are
I don't know your company
I don't know your company's product
I don't know what your company stands for
I don't know your company's customers
I don't know your company's record
I don't know your company's reputation
Now – what was it you wanted to sell me?

My thanks to David Peoples for
his inspiration, Jeff Leviss for his
support and to my wife and
daughter for their patience.

Copyright © Nigel Henzell-Thomas

First published in Great Britain by
Business Books Limited
An imprint of Century Hutchinson Limited
62–65 Chandos Place, London, WC2N 4NW

Century Hutchinson Australia (Pty) Limited
89–91 Albion Street, Surry Hills,
New South Wales 2010, Australia

Century Hutchinson New Zealand Limited
PO Box 40–086, 3234 View Road, Glenfield,
Auckland 10, New Zealand

Century Hutchinson South Africa (Pty) Limited
PO Box 337, Bergvlei 2012, South Africa

Certain passages in this book are based upon material
developed for IBM Corporation and IBM UK Limited and
are reproduced with permission from those companies.

Text on page 6 reproduced with permission from McGraw
Hill Inc.

British Library Cataloguing in Publication Data
Henzell – Thomas, Nigel
Supercharge your selling.
1. Salesmanship
I. Title
658.8'5

ISBN 0-09-174231-5

CONTENTS

Contents

PART TWO: Pre-Sales

Contents

PART THREE: The Sales Call

Contents

Contents

PART FOUR: After-Sales

Contents

Contents

PART SIX: To Close

INTRODUCTION

Welcome to **Supercharge your Selling** – 60 Tips in 60 Minutes. The objective of this book is to help you to achieve incremental business, with much less effort, by making sure that you do all the right things the very first time. The rules of the game say that if you get that sales call wrong the first time, then it'll cost you ten times as much in terms of your time to put it right. And if you get it wrong a second time, then it'll cost you one hundred times as much!

There must have been many times when you have resolutely gone out to buy something for the house or the office only to meet a salesperson who, by employing the most extraordinary of sales techniques, manages to convince you to think again!

Have you ever asked yourself how many of your customers and prospects are approached by you and receive similar treatment?

Why does one salesperson close an order when another fails? It's really that magic spark that makes an individual say or do the right thing at the right time that wins the sale. Alfred Tack once said that a truly great salesperson is that man or woman who is able to use a hundred or more very small, unexceptional ideas, but to use them so effectively that the whole becomes an outstandingly good sale. He was right! And if **you** get it right, that's not only good for you, but also good for the company for which you work.

I hope that this book will not only give you some useful and valid tips and techniques to ensure that you stay in front of the selling race but that it will also demonstrate that selling, whilst being a serious business, can also be a business where an element of good-natured humour exists.

Why is humour so important? Because we're in danger of becoming exceedingly boring in the way in which we conduct our discussions with our prospects and customers. Many of them are often confounded – certainly in technical environments – by our business proposals and they yearn to do business with enthusiastic and convincing salespeople, rather than with those who are skilled in advanced techniques of boredom and logic.

The skills that you have today are the result of the decisions that you made yesterday.

The skills that you'll have tomorrow could be the result of decisions that you make as a result of reading this book.

You only need to refresh your mind with one or two things that you might have forgotten or learn one or two things of which you were previously unaware for you to recoup your outlay many times over.

Whether you are in management or otherwise, in whichever company you work, performing whatever function, never forget that you represent your company as a 'salesperson' in one guise or another.

I wish you the greatest success.

Nigel Henzell-Thomas.

PART ONE

THE ENVIRONMENT IN WHICH YOU WORK

TIP 1 Call on the Managing Director

This is undoubtedly the single most important tip. If you are successful at it, then you will be confirmed as a great salesperson. It's so important that there is nothing that comes a close second. Of all the things that there are to know, if you follow this first tip, then I guarantee that you will be successful.

More often than not, they are actually easy to see. They are certainly the easiest to talk with. They let you know within the first few minutes whether or not you're wasting your time but, above all, they're decision-makers. How often have you heard a Managing Director say 'it's not in the budget', or 'I don't have the authority'!

The hardest person to talk to is the Accountant. Even worse, the Assistant Accountant. They're book-keepers. And even if you are successful in selling to the book-keeper, he or she then has to sell to the Managing Director. The problem is that, if book-keepers could sell, they wouldn't be book-keepers. Accountants view all proposals as a cost and there are few accountants who like costs.

So, double your sales and double your money:

Call on the Managing Director.

T_{IP} *2* *What Next?*

Tip 2 is so important that, other than Tip 1, it's the most important thing that you need to know about selling.

If you can be successful at Tip 2, then you will gain a reputation and a level of credibility that will be difficult to beat.

You will have outstanding customer references, making it easier for you to open new accounts.

Tip 2 is:

Call on the Managing Director!

TIP 3 *Be a Specialist*

This is the age of the expert. If you try to be all things to all people, you'll be nothing. You'll spread your talent too thinly.

The person with the need and the money will gladly pay a premium to increase the probability of success and reduce the risk of failure. And that comes from doing business with those people who have the experience, common sense and references in their corner of the world.

The 1990s will see the growth and prospering of the niche marketer. So find that part of the business in which you feel most comfortable and confident and gain that experience and make those references.

TIP 4 *Don't be an Inventor,*
                Don't be a Pioneer

You won't win any prizes and you'll finish the year poorer than when you began.

Concentrate on those things where you know that you have a chance of success. Let your competitors be side-tracked by those obscure requests that will take up inordinate amounts of their time and bring them little reward.

Learn to say 'no' at the outset. Explain that you and your company do not possess this or that level of expertise to solve the problem (or request) that has been presented by your customer or prospect. Alternatively, call in that part of your company that does possess the skills and experience to present an acceptable solution.

. Use your time effectively. Don't be unnecessarily side-tracked.

TIP **5** *Follow Pareto's Law*

Once upon a time, an Italian economist and political philosopher called Vilfredo Pareto observed that within a given population, the distribution of income remained proportionately constant whatever efforts were made to change it. This 80/20 rule has been found to apply to many other areas as well, including selling. What this means to you is that just as 20% of the 'Pareto's population' always had 80% of the money, you will find that 80% of your money comes from 20% of your customers.

So be sure that you spend 80% of your time with the 20% that pays your mortgage and buys the food.

In this way, you'll be one of the 20% with 80% of the money!

Remember this 80/20 rule and follow Pareto's Law.

Part Two

PART TWO

PRE-SALES

TIP 6

Attend a Course on Presentation Skills

How would you like to earn at least 40% more money in the next twelve months?

Statistically, I could probably prove that if you successfully complete such a course, you will actually earn considerably more than the person sitting next to you in your office who has not taken that opportunity.

In addition, you'll stand out in any crowd because one of the weaknesses in all people is their presentation and speaking ability, with the single greatest fear of humans being speaking before a group.

This is substantiated by a survey in the United States where people were asked the ten things that they most feared. In ascending order, they were: dogs, loneliness, flying, death, sickness, deep water, financial problems, insects and bugs, heights and, **top of the list**, speaking before a group!

Anyone can learn to present effectively to other people. However, few people naturally possess strong presentation skills. Consider some of the following key elements of effective presentations:

● **Eye Contact**. Repeated eye contact significantly increases the attentiveness, involvement and interest of your audience. Do you ensure that you look at all members of your audience, giving one complete sentence or thought, and then move on?

- **Gestures**. Do you use natural and relaxed gestures to add emphasis to the points that you are making?

- **Poise**. The confidence that is displayed by you will often make or break your presentation. Standing straight, yet relaxed, is an example of poised behaviour.

- **Control**. A good presenter is always aware of the audience and has control of the presentation. When the audience appears to be distracted or to have lost interest, do you move closer to them, perhaps even using exaggerated gestures, to regain their attention? Do you smile? Not only with your lips, but also with your eyes? Do you let your face communicate, as well as your words, the exciting benefits of your proposal?

If these aren't familiar to you, it's time for you to improve your presentation skills. Competence in this area will make you a very successful salesperson.

Go to Tip 55 for some additional self-assessment and to learn how effective you really are today.

TIP 7 Motivate and Train your Support People

Information about your customer is a crucial asset. For example, in the Personal Computer business, how useful is it to know that your customer's existing installation is giving unexpected problems? How useful is it to know that a customer with a single machine has purchased significant/additional software over a three month period?

So **motivate and train your support people** to recognize this type of information as a strong signal for a potential sale and make sure it gets passed on to you.

This will make your telephone calls to your customers very powerful: you'll be referring to something that your customer has done, indicating your interest in them, and demonstrating real customer care.

In any purchase decision, buyers go through six steps:

1) they develop an **awareness** of what's available.
2) They seek out **knowledge** about the different products and services on offer.
3) They develop **likes** for certain products and services and eliminate those they don't like
4) They develop a **preference**
5) They develop a **conviction** about buying that preference
6) They purchase that **preference**

These phases are the same the world over, irrespective of the product or service being purchased. The question is, 'Can you afford to spend time on a one-to-one basis going through each step?' For those really big decisions, of course. But for those other decisions the answer's no!

Use direct marketing to cost-effectively address the first four steps and limit your personal selling to the conviction and purchase stages. Sales prospecting, without qualified leads, is both time-consuming and expensive. Expensive for you and expensive for your company.

How do you do it? By direct mail, telemarketing, seminars, advertising and trade shows.

In today's competitive environment, you must be innovative in these marketing techniques to ensure that you and your company stand out from the crowd.

TIP 9 *Prepare References*

There's only one thing that's a better advertisement than a happy customer and that's a happy customer who's prepared to tell everybody.

Determine your best customer references and write them as though the Managing Directors of the companies concerned were telling the story. Focus on the old way versus the new way, the benefits and the cash savings.

Gain agreement from the respective managing directors for you to use these reference sheets in your mail-shot campaigns.

It costs a fraction of the cost of advertising and you will achieve increased sales through your increased level of professionalism. It also brings to you and your company a high level of credibility in any sales situation.

And for some icing on the cake, go to Tip 10.

TIP *10* *Target Your Mail Shots*

Target that mail shot to the narrowest possible audience. A shotgun approach will bring you less than a one per cent response. Don't waste your time on such a blanket cover nor waste the valuable time of those who support you in preparing your mail shots. If you're truly motivating them, you'll be telling them the results of all the contributory work that they do and I can tell you that a one per cent response rate is not something likely to spur them on! You will be wasting not only your own time but also theirs.

So target your mail shot at a *specific* audience, carrying a *specific* message. You'll not only receive a far higher response rate, but the quality of response will be exceptional owing to the fact that the companies that respond will believe that you have a solution that is unique to them.

This tip alone could well be worth the time, and associated costs, that you have put aside to read this book.

You know you should be doing business with the Managing Director, but more often than not, when you ring, the secretary is reluctant to put you through: secretaries are expert at protecting their bosses. If you write, you may well not receive a response.

So why not make a tape of your sales presentation? Use it to tell these Managing Directors why you want to see them and what's in it for them and their companies.

You don't need to get a production company to prepare it. Do it yourself: just make a cassette of you talking. In the majority of cases, Managing Directors will be intrigued by such an innovative and novel way of presenting a sales case. You will also have their undivided attention!

They'll want to meet you. Money can't buy an opportunity like that and you're on the way to differentiating yourself and your company from all the rest.

TIP *12* *Improve Your Telephone Techniques*

How many telephone calls do you need to make an appointment? If it's ten calls for one appointment, how do you feel about wasting 90% of your time? The solution is simple:

Attend a course on telephone skills.

Even if you only improve your number of appointments to one more out of ten, you've doubled your productivity and reduced your rejection rate.

You'll learn that you must first sell the appointment and then, and only then, sell your product and services during the meeting itself. The telephone call is the sale before the sale and there's only one objective – to sell the sales interview – not your product or service.

Making that telephone call for an appointment is a skill and I can guarantee that 90% of us are bad at it.

And the other 10%? They've attended a course on the effective use of the telephone in making appointments.

PART THREE

THE SALES CALL

TIP *13* *Appointment Times*

Try making that appointment at times other than on the hour or half hour.

Make that appointment for ten-past-five rather than five, for twenty-past-two rather than two-thirty. By making an appointment for that time you are indicating that you are there for a short meeting. The prospect has a reasonable expectation that you will finish at five-forty-five or three o'clock in the above examples.

People in authority like that. It sets the scene. Here am I, the Managing Director of my company, about to meet busy salespeople, people who work to a tight schedule and whose customers can only let them go at odd times during the day. Maybe they have something important to say. That's why their other customers decided to go ahead and perhaps that's why I should listen to them.

It's undoubtedly the single most important tip and if you are successful at it, then you will be confirmed as a great salesperson. It's so important that there is nothing that comes a close second.

Of all the things there are to know, if you follow this tip, then I guarantee that you will be successful.

Call on the Managing Director.

More often than not, they are actually easier to see. They are certainly the easiest to talk with. They let you know within the first few minutes whether or not you're wasting your time but, above all, they're decision makers. How often have you heard a Managing Director say 'it's not in the budget' or 'I don't have the authority'!

So, call on the Managing Director and double your sales and double your money.

TIP 15 *Dress for Success*

Is appearance important?

Of course it is. You, the salesperson, are the company. You're responsible for creating your company's image in the buyer's mind.

Often-quoted examples are those of the Managing Directors of chocolate and shoe manufacturers. In the case of the former, they'll be conscious about hygiene, looking at your fingertips with a microscopic interest. In the case of the latter, you'd reduce any chance of success by orders of magnitude if you didn't polish your shoes!

When you don't get the order, you're rarely, if ever, told the real reason. They're not going to look you in the eye and tell you that they don't do business with people who wear yellow shirts or white socks. They'll say, instead, 'Your price is too high'.

If you're a comedian, wear white socks. Unless you're a comedian, dress conservatively. Wear a dark suit, white shirt and that conservative tie. Save those pastels and polka dots for the coffee club and not for the Managing Director.

It's often said that a sale is made in the first few seconds of the call. That's a lie. It's lost, not made, in the first few seconds. Remember you never get a second chance to make a first impression.

TIP 16 *Set Yourself Objectives*

If you don't know where you're going, you'll never get there.

Making a sales call is like going on a journey with your customer in the passenger seat. It's inconceivable that you would start the engine without having agreed with the passenger about where you are both going. This is called 'setting mutually agreeable objectives'.

Occasionally, during the journey, you'll stop and check where you are. You'll take a look at a map. This is called 'summarizing and establishing the next step'.

Often, when I'm in a sales office, I hear salespeople discussing calls that they've made and one will ask the other 'How did it go?' The answer is often along the lines 'Very well. We had a good chat. We got on famously. Things are progressing.'

Objectives are therefore statements of *end-results* to be achieved within a given period of time. Note the stress on end-results. A list of activities to be undertaken is not to be confused with objective setting. This list of activities should be called a plan and it's desirable to set plans for objectives.

● Endeavour to set an objective for each indicator.

- Objectives should be set in terms of the results to be achieved (occasionally, a task can be used as an objective).
- Make your objectives difficult, but attainable.
- State your objectives precisely, preferably in measurable form.
- Your objectives should be practical in use. Restrict them to important results.
- See Tip 17: MAKE THEM EXCITING!

The simple truth is that if you fail to set an objective for the call, there's never a danger of your failing to meet that objective.

So, in addition to your setting an objective for every call that you make, it's also good practice to ask yourself three other questions:

- When I see my prospects, *what are the benefits* that will accrue to them as a result of seeing me?
- *Why would they want* to accept my proposals?
- *What else* could I be doing that would help them on the way to a positive decision?

To make an effective sales campaign and be an effective salesperson, you have to be able to positively answer these questions before you make your calls.

TIP 17
Learn to Run a Successful Seminar

To sell effectively, you need the means to put a clear sales message in front of groups of customers and potential customers. By running a business seminar specially tailored for your customers' areas of interest, you create an unrivalled opportunity to explain your products or services in depth.

Seminars, when run well, provide you with detailed feedback on your customers' real needs and attitudes – valuable input to your marketing planning.

Your prospective customers also benefit from a well-organized seminar. It provides them with sound information in their sphere of interest, the chance to discuss (both with you and with fellow attendees) their needs for today's organization and future growth, to develop a close-up view of the available products or services and to understand the associated benefits.

For greatest effect, the seminar should address a specific business need. This enables you to structure your seminar for the highest levels of presentation. Use existing customers to present on your behalf. Prospective customers believe other customers.

The key to success depends on setting realistic objectives and planning to meet these objectives. There are a few musts:

- The objectives must be exciting.
- The objectives must be measurable over the short-term.
- The objectives must be measurable quantitively. Set yourself a target!

TIP 18 *Learn to Listen*

Many individuals neglect this most important communication skill.

Few of us realize that we spend an average of 80% of our working day communicating. Of this communication time, 9% is spent writing, 16% reading, 30% talking and 45% listening.

Immediately after hearing something, most of us can recall only 50% of what we heard. Within two to eight weeks, we can recall only 25% or less of the original message. Our mental attitudes reduce our ability to retain what we hear.

Some guides to being a good listener:

● *STOP TALKING* – you can't listen whilst you are talking.
● *ASK QUESTIONS* – when you don't understand, when you need further clarification, when you want them to like you and when you want to show that you are listening.
● *DON'T INTERRUPT* – give them time to say what they have to say.
● *CONCENTRATE ON WHAT THEY ARE SAYING* – actively focus your attention on their words, their ideas and their feelings as they relate to the subject.
● *LOOK AT THE PROSPECT* – their face, their mouth, their eyes and their hands will help them to communicate with you. By looking,

it also gives them confidence that you are, in fact, listening. It helps you to concentrate too.

● *LEAVE YOUR EMOTIONS BEHIND (if you can)* – try to forget your own worries and problems. Leave them outside of the meeting room. They'll prevent you from listening well.

● *UNDERSTAND THE MAIN POINTS* – concentrate on the main ideas and not the illustrative material. Examples, stories and statistics are important but are usually not the main points. Examine them only to see if they prove, support or define the main ideas.

● *REACT TO IDEAS, NOT TO PEOPLE* – don't allow your reactions to the person to influence your interpretation of what he or she says. Their ideas might be excellent and you should not be swayed by the fact that you dislike them as individuals or the way that they look.

● *DON'T ARGUE MENTALLY* – when you are trying to understand other people, it's a handicap to argue with them mentally as they are speaking. This only sets up a barrier between yourself and the speaker.

● *USE THE DIFFERENCE IN RATE* – you can listen faster than you can talk. So use this rate difference to your advantage by: staying on the right track, anticipating what they are going to say, thinking back over what they have just said and evaluating the development of their argument. You speak at about 100 to 150 words per minute, but you think at 250 to 500.

● *LISTEN FOR WHAT IS NOT SAID* – sometimes you can learn just as much by determining what other people leave out or avoid in their conversation as you can by listening to what they say.

● *LISTEN TO HOW SOMETHING IS SAID* – we frequently concentrate so hard on what is said that we miss the importance of the emotional reactions and attitudes as they relate to what is said. Often, these attitudes and emotional reactions may be more important than what is said in so many words.

● AVOID JUMPING TO ASSUMPTIONS – they can get you into trouble in trying to understand other people. Don't assume that they use words the same way that you do; that they didn't say what they meant, but you understood what they meant; that they are distorting the truth because what they say doesn't agree with what you think; that they are lying because they have interpreted the facts differently from the way you have. Assumptions such as these may turn out to be true, but more often than not, they just get in the way of your understanding and reaching agreement or compromise.

Learn to listen!

Ten reasons why.

- *To open discussion* – After you have made your opening remarks, you will find the opening for that first question: a general question, 'What . . .?' 'Why . . .?', 'How . . .?', 'Where . . .?', 'Who . . .?'
- *To develop understanding* – Help your prospects to recall essential data. Ask questions that yield information: 'What budget do you have to resolve these problems?'
- *To stimulate thinking* – Good questions generate the interest and curiosity necessary for thinking and learning. They arouse the curiosity and and desire to explore the problem further: 'When do you think that increase in demand will take place?'
- *To direct thinking* – If the discussion seems to be going off track, questions serve the purpose of directing thinking back to the point in hand: 'How would you answer that?' 'In terms of my proposal, what effect do you think that that would have?'
- *To accumulate data* – Questions seeking facts, data, information: 'How many . . .?'
- *To develop a subject* – Phrase ideas in the form of a question, and so make the development of your subject more subtle: 'To what extent does . . .?

● *To change the trend in discussion* – A properly chosen question can bring the thinking of your prospect into another element of the subject: 'What's your thinking on this part of my proposal?'
● *To arrive at a summary* – Use questions to check for progress and understanding. A good question will tell you if you are on target and give you a summary: 'Where between these points of view that we've discussed does our course of action lie?'
● *To ask how strong an argument is* – 'How much importance do you think we should attach to this requirement?'
● *To suggest that all info has been given* – 'What information can you give me at this point in addition to that which has alraedy been given?'

TIP 20

Use Those Key Words When Questioning

The question is one of the keys to human behaviour, achievement and co-operation. It unlocks the problems that we experience during the sales call and it takes time and practice to develop the ability to ask the right question of the right person at the right time.

There are some key words that you can use in your questions on your calls, each of which requires those being questioned to respond in a particular manner, as described below. Your prospect's answers will enable you to be more effective in your sales campaigns.

- **Classify** requires the prospect to assemble and group facts in relation to the subject
- **Compare** requires the prospect to detect the similarity and difference amongst facts
- **Define** asks the prospect to determine the limits to a subject and fix a clear meaning
- **Describe** asks the prospect to select features or qualities which characterize a subject, situation or action
- **Explain** asks the prospect to clarify any points which may be obscuring the subject

- **Illustrate** requires the prospect to give examples that will clear up the subject under consideration

- **Interpret** asks the prospect to bring out the meaning of a subject using their judgment

- **Outline** requires the prospect to give an oral sketching of a situation and its significance

- **Review** the prospect is compelled to go over a subject deliberately, giving it a critical examination

- **Summarize** requires the prospect to present his problem (for example) in a concise and compact manner

- **Trace** asks the prospect to explain in detail the development or the progress of a subject.

Don't forget that the prospect can also ask YOU these questions about your proposals, so be prepared!

TIP 21
Learn to Frame Your Questions

- *Plan your questions.* Make them trace the line of thought you plan to follow.
- *Make the wording definite, clear and concise.* Your prospects prefer to know exactly what they are being asked. There should be no ambiguity.
- *Make each question centre on only one idea.* Do not combine two or three questions in one.
- *Take into consideration your perception as to your prospects knowledge.* At first, adapt your questions according to your perception of his or her ability and experience.
- *Allow for subsidiary questions.* If your question is one that requires thought, replies that are very prompt often indicate that very little thinking has taken place on your prospect's part. Ensure that you follow-up by asking subsidiary questions to force your prospect to fully review the points under discussion. Their prompt response may be right, but don't risk it!
- *Use What?, Why?, When?, How?, Where?, and Who?*

We kept six honest working men
They taught us all we know
Their names are WHAT and WHY and WHEN
And HOW and WHERE and WHO

TIP *22* *Learn How to Summarize*

Whenever you leave a meeting with your prospects, you should leave them with the feeling that something has been accomplished. Conclusions should be clear and definite. You should have summarized the highlights of your discussion and emphasized the major conclusions that have been agreed.

- Use simple words
- Use phrases and short sentences
- State each step briefly
- Put steps, or points, brought out in the meeting in the right order.
- Differentiate between each point so that the prospect gets one point at a time
- Should you be summarizing to a group, it may be appropriate to mention who in the group brought up a particular point
- Speak slowly so that each point and the general meaning has a chance to sink in
- Don't hesitate to get the commitment of the prospect to take positive action on your proposal if that's what is required.

TIP 23 Learn When to Summarize

Learning 'how' is just part of it. Understanding 'when' is just as important.

- At the end of your presentation – just before the discussion
- When the discussion on your proposal gets off track
- When all the points of one part of your proposal or phase have been raised
- When the discussion has brought out all possible objections and the time has come for the prospect to make a decision
- When the prospect has reached a positive decision and there is the requirement to agree on how best to implement your proposal

And when you have that agreement to go ahead, conclude that meeting in the most credible manner.

- Thank them for placing their order with your company
- Conclude the meeting as naturally as it was started
- Don't keep your prospect talking too long once agreement has been reached. They have other things to do. If you've been professional in your summarizing skills, they'll have a

clear understanding of the benefits of your proposal. Don't overdo it!

As you present more and more to a prospect group from one company, you'll find that you are dealing with several different individuals. One of your main objectives must be to get participation from the entire group – to hold down the most talkative and build up the silent. In that way, you will be sure to gain the agreement of all the group to your proposals, having understood and answered all their objections, rather than those that were voiced by the most vociferous.

Let's look at some of the different types that you will meet and some remedies.

● *Those who talk too much*: often these people are so eager that they don't realize that they are doing it.
   ... and the remedy: slow them down with summary statements and direct your next question to someone else.
● *Those who know all the answers*: They may think they know the answer to the problem better than anyone else. They feel that they are really trying to help, but in the process make it difficult for their colleagues to participate.
   ... and the remedy: endeavour to cut across such an individual by questioning others. Use him or her for summarizing.

Learn to Handle Prospects During Your Presentation

● *Those who want to argue*: with these people, nothing about your proposal is right. They will criticize everything.

... *and the remedy*: reword or rephrase their criticisms to make them appear more acceptable. Try to find merit in one of their points. Above all, control yourself.

● *Those who talk to their colleagues*: these people do not have the courage of their convictions to say what they want openly.

... *and the remedy*: you naturally don't want to embarrass them. Endeavour to ask them to comment on an easily understandable part of your proposal. Do it after a summary so that they have a 'prompt'.

● *Those that won't talk*: they may be bored, indifferent, feel superior or insecure. Or they may not recognize the benefits to be gained from your proposals.

... *and the remedy*: use direct questions calling upon their 'experience'. Ask for their comments on your proposal, 'What do you think? . . .'

● *Those who are wrong in their comments*: they're mistaken, but their colleagues in the room fail to correct them. Their comments are obviously incorrect.

... *and the remedy*: delicate handling is required. You must avoid direct criticism.

You could correct them indirectly by an analysis of similar situations where there have been proven successes.

By an understanding of the different types of individuals that you will meet, you will not only improve your presentation skills but also improve your close rate.

TIP 25

Don't Talk About Yourself

When I was younger, I remember going to parties where I would find myself chatting to a really attractive woman in the certain knowledge that I was telling her some really interesting things about myself . . . my job, my hobbies, my car and my holidays.

There was nothing more devastating than the growing realization that this beautiful woman did not suffer from some unfortunate squint, but rather that her eyes had wandered to some other person strategically placed past my left ear.

So I asked myself, 'What is the definition of a bore?' and I decided that the following definition was the most appropriate:

Someone who talks about themselves when you want to talk about yourself.

So Tip 25 is don't talk about yourself, your company or your products or services; ask your customers questions about themselves, their company and their requirements.

That's how to be an interesting and successful salesperson.

When you call on your prospects and customers, you should reflect on what they have to go through during the call. You're not the only one working very hard. They have to be just as agile during the sale as you have to be in your sales presentation.

- They will want to understand the benefits that are contained within your proposal.
- They will want to seek clarification of the points that you are making.
- They will want to relate your proposals to their requirements and needs.
- They will want to compare your proposals with those of your competitor.
- They will want examples of similar successful sales that you have made.
- They will have to consider your company's reputation.
- They will have to decide as to whether they should do business with you.
- They will have to form an opinion of YOU.

So Tip 26 is give your prospects a helping hand. Understand that they also have to think during the call.

If you know what they are going through, then it makes sense for you to use this knowledge during your call. For example, 'Am I

clearly stating the benefits of my proposal?',
'Am I giving prospects the opportunity to state
their objections?', 'Is my proposal really competitive?', 'Do I have some good references to
hand?', 'Can I successfully demonstrate my
company's track record?', 'Am I presenting
myself in a businesslike, though likeable
manner?'

TIP 27 *Sell Solutions*

People buy benefits not features, so sell benefits. Be a cook and not a saucepan salesperson.

What you sell is that good night's sleep: peace and tranquility, tonight, tomorrow and forever!

The prospects won't confess it, but that's what they really want. Transition to your proposed new world without heart attacks, divorce or blood on the floor. That £1,000 or £20,000 saving is forgotten within moments of the saving being made and, in three years' time, when things start to go wrong, they'll be after you.

So focus your sales strategy on selling your competence, your experience, your trade record and your control of the business. This means in every discussion that you have, in every proposal that you write, you must include three main elements that prove not only your own commitment to your proposals, but also that of the management to whom you are proposing:

● Education and training.
● Implementation planning and progress meetings or whatever reviews are appropriate.
● Management involvement – in every authoritative study that has ever been done, when looking for the common denominator between success and failure, the conclusion has always been the same. The critical factor,

the common denominator, is management
involvement in the implementation of your
proposals.

TIP 28

Have Three Prices, Not One

If you have problems selling the added cost of service that your company provides, then this tip is the answer:

People in business like to have a choice, so give them a choice.

- Price A – Bare bones proposal, minimum support.

- Price B – Your normal way of doing business including the standard level of support.

- Price C – A turnkey job, including detailed training proposals and a level of service above that which is normally given.

Use your own words to differentiate your offerings.

Even if you never get any takers on A and C, you'll sell more of B because you offered three. It could be that it's the one you want to sell anyway.

TIP 29
Don't Give Demonstrations

That's right, on complex products, don't give demonstrations unless you really have to.

If your prospects had any doubt about the product before your demonstration, then, after your demonstration, they'll be left in no doubt that:

A – they don't understand the product or the technology.

B – their companies don't have the ability to install it.

In addition, most people are not very good at it. They demonstrate features without stressing the benefits. They ask people to attend demonstrations without having questioned, established needs and agreed those needs. They therefore introduce the demonstration into the sales cycle far too early, resulting in an inconsequential and unproductive event.

If your prospects are really serious, sooner or later they'll want to visit a company that has one in their industry doing their job.

So, don't waste your time. Send them to a good reference. Let satisfied users do your selling for you. They have a credibility that you don't have and you'll get the order in less time with half the effort. Moreover, it'll be better sold and stay sold.

Often, salespeople say that there were times when they failed to get an order that should have been theirs.

In hindsight, they know that there have been opportunities that they've missed because they didn't emphasize the positive qualities of their own company's support and confirm that company's management involvement.

When a competitor was talking to that same prospect, offering that identical solution, but emphasizing their support, then it is not unnatural that these salespeople lost out.

How are you going to counter this?

Early on in the sales cycle, the Managing Director should clearly understand that, of your successful sales, every one has been successful except three. The common denominator in all three cases was the absence of top management involvement, confirming our experience and the conclusion of every independent study looking for the key factor that makes the difference between success and failure in making progress.

In fact, if you should ever meet an unhappy customer, just ask one question, 'What was the degree of involvement of top management?'

If you were to play roulette, how would you like to place your money on a number knowing that it was the winning number?

You can do that by helping your prospects to do some comparison shopping.

Give them a check-list of things to compare. Don't leave it to chance. If you define the rules, you'll win the game.

So give them a list of your strengths and suggest that they compare on those items.

TIP 32

Publicize Your Company Team

If I was your competitor, I'd tell your prospects that you don't know how to support your customers.

How do you counter this? In every situation, you give the Managing Director the name, title and telephone number of *key* people in your company who have a vested interest in the success and satisfaction of their company. Include a list, again with telephone numbers, of all those people in your company whose success and future is related to their satisfaction.

Have to hand a copy of the original version of 'There's no such thing as a free lunch'.

People make decisions emotionally and then justify them with logic. They know first that they want to do it and then they justify that decision.

And the man or woman who wants to do business with you can justify anything whilst the man or woman who doesn't want to do business with you cannot justify anything.

So, when a prospect or customer says that you're too expensive, ask whether he wants the cheapest solution or the best value for money.

Price should not be the primary consideration. It's value for money that counts. Your role is to outweigh price with benefits.

John Ruskin died 89 years ago, but there's hardly a day that goes by without someone quoting a shortened version of what he wrote.

This version says, 'There's no such thing as a free lunch.'

The original version really spells it out. Give your customers and prospects a copy, or, even better, have it printed on a card.

The 1980s and 1990s version of this statement will be that there is no such thing as free service from any professional marketing company.

COMMON SENSE VS NONSENSE
'It's unwise to pay too much, but it's worse to

pay too little. When you pay too much, you lose a little money – that is all. When you pay too little, you sometimes lose everything, because the thing you bought was incapable of doing the thing it was bought to do. The common law of business balance prohibits paying a little and getting a lot – it can't be done. If you deal with the lowest bidder, it is well to add something for the risk you run, and if you do that you will have enough to pay for something better.'

John Ruskin
(1819–1900)

TIP 34
Implement 50% Ahead of Schedule

It's so easy, takes no more effort and nothing pleases a customer more than a job finished ahead of schedule.

But how do you do it? It's simple. Allow for contingencies and tell your prospects and customers that the job will take longer than you think it will. Tell them that any competitor who claims otherwise will simply be unable to do the quality of job required for a successful implementation.

There are often unforeseen hurdles. Allow for them in the schedule and then ensure that they don't happen. So they win and you win and that's called win-win.

There are no losers in the win-win game.

Some business is not worth having. It costs you more in time, trouble and money than you ever get out of it.

Tip 35 is KNOW WHEN TO GIVE UP. If they aren't willing to comply with your requirements for a successful installation (whether product or service), as described in Tip 27, that is, education and training, planning and progress meetings and management involvement, then follow your instincts and walk away.

And remember to take them off your prospect list. There is now no justifiable reason for them to be included.

TIP 36 *Qualify Your Prospects*

You will never be a successful salesperson unless you qualify your prospect. Despite the fact that salespeople's time is their most valuable commodity, why do so many waste their time chasing a 'wish list' that has no substance?

There is no merit in covering your quota with prospects that you know, in your heart of hearts, will never place an order with you.

So ask yourself some leading questions regarding your prospect list:

- Am I talking to the decision-maker, influencer or information collector.
- If not a decision-maker, who is the decision-maker and have I arranged to see him or her?
- What is the date of their decision?
- Has a budget been approved and how much is it?
- What are the key buying criteria? Should I add some key criteria?
- What is my probability of winning?
- What is my competition?
- What specific support is required by the company to close the order?

If you are not in a position to review these questions in a positive manner, then, believe me, you do not have a worthwhile prospect list.

Learn to Use the 12 Most Persuasive Words in the English Language.

According to a University study, they are:

● You
● Money
● Save
● New
● Results
● Easy
● Health
● Safety
● Have
● Discovery
● Proven
● Guarantee

When someone hears these words, they would appear to provide certain personal benefits or advantages.

Incorporate them in your presentations and discussions!

Now that your customers are going to install ahead of schedule, Tip 38 is:

CONFIRM THAT DECISION TO DO BUSINESS WITH YOU

Confirm it during your sales call. Buyers will always have concerns once they've made that decision to buy. More often than not, this state of mind occurs owing to the fact that each of the options that the buyer considers has features, functions and benefits that are attractive.

Whilst we would like to think that perfect solutions exist, in reality they seldom do. Therefore, when prospects decide to go ahead with your proposals, they do so in the clear understanding that, there being no perfect solution, your proposals may have some limitations. Prospects will also be aware that the other proposals that they considered, and decided against, may well have had some benefits. Naturally, however, in selecting your proposal, the prospect has chosen the option with the greatest number of benefits overall.

Prospects may, therefore, spend a great deal of time evaluating the options to ensure that their decision is the most appropriate to meet their needs.

Confirm it when you close the order. Confirm your company's reputation and it's track record, confirm your company's after-sales service, confirm that back-up team and confirm your proven commitment to your customers.

Confirm it when you install or implement your solution.

Confirm that decision on a regular basis thereafter.

When you close an order, capitalize on that success on your next appointment.

Many salespeople actually cancel their next appointment so that they can get back to the office with their order. They take all that excitement and dispel it in their office rather than with another prospect.

They not only miss a marvellous opportunity but they are in danger of becoming poor performers!

TIP 40
Don't Just Say 'I'll be Right There'

We've already agreed that we all have an equal amount of time during the day and the key is how effective we can be in the use of that time.

ASK YOURSELF SOME HARD QUESTIONS BEFORE YOU SAY YOU'LL BE RIGHT THERE

● Could the person best see someone else?
● Could I handle this by telephone or letter?
● Will I be seeing the right person?
● Do I have a good reason to be there?
● Am I prepared?
● Is a return trip required?
● Do I have an appointment?

Whenever customers want to see you, always ask them what they want to see you about! On many occasions, they don't want to see you at all. They want to be introduced to some other person in your organization.

PART FOUR

AFTER-SALES

There's another way to earn the respect of your customer.

You do it by focusing your thoughts on the one thing on which no other salesperson has concentrated.

For all the other salespeople, a customer request has been put in the queue along with all the other things that they l ave to do. They get around to it a week, ten days or two weeks later.

When a customer asks you to do something, do it Right Now!

What is it that you are doing right now that is more important than earning the respect of your customers?

So Tip 41, rephrased, is

If you can't get back right away and even if you don't have the answer, let your customers and prospects know what you're doing and why they're waiting.

The one single biggest factor that makes one salesperson stand apart from another is responsiveness. So differentiate yourself from your competitors by responding to your customers and prospects.

One golden rule of all relationships is that people like pleasant surprises but hate nasty surprises. This is one area where 'killing the messenger' is the norm.

Problems don't just go away. They tend to get bigger and bigger. You can't hide a giraffe. So discuss the problem early and tell the truth.

It all adds up to increasing your credibility and professionalism as a salesperson and people will want to do business with you.

TIP 43 — Write to Your Existing Customers

The professional company always maintains executive contact. So, at least once a year, ensure that your Managing Director *sends a letter to all of your existing customers.*

- Thank them for being a customer.
- Tell them how important they are to the company.
- Thank them for the business and for the opportunity to work with them.
- Tell them of the improvements that have been made to better support them.
- Tell them of your company's thoughts and plans for the following year.

More often than not, your customers don't realize all the things that your company has done and the progress that it's made over the last year unless you tell them.

So, thank them for the business, tell them again how important they are and provide that professional platform for more follow-up business.

The only birthday card (other than from family) that most people receive is one from their insurance broker. If they are particularly lucky, they'll get one from their bank manager.

Send a birthday card to your customers on the anniversary of that major sale.

This helps keep a reference and provides that perfect opportunity for follow-up business.

TIP 45
That Token of Appreciation

Taking delivery of your product or service should be like taking delivery of the new car that you've been looking forward to.

It's a significant event and, for some companies, it could be the biggest event of the year. So make it a big event! Send some flowers to the staff, with an appropriate message, on the day that the product is installed or that new service is introduced. If flowers do not appeal to you, find something that does.

But to make the relationship last for ever, go to Tip 46.

Take out your camera, or get a photographer, and give your customers and prospects a lifetime memory of the big event – a picture of the Managing Director (or whoever) standing beside the new installation of your company's product or a group engaged in lively discussion regarding your service that they have just introduced.

Get the picture enlarged and framed, presenting it at an appropriate occasion.

TIP 47

Be a Good Friend to Your Support Team

Salespeople come and salespeople go but the support and technical teams keep the account together. Don't alienate them!

In most cases, they know more about the account than you do. Your customers probably trust them more than you.

Support teams tell you who's who and who's not, what to do and what to look out for.

As your part of the bargain, you'll explain your account strategy so that they understand your direction and can support you when they are in your account.

Let your support teams be your back-up salespeople, albeit in different clothing.

PART FIVE

YOU!

There are problems on every territory and I can assure you that there are no good or bad territories – only good or bad salespeople.

NEVER COMPLAIN ABOUT YOUR ACCOUNTS OR TERRITORY

There are sales to be made in every territory and the next time that you want to blame your patch, just remember that there are thousands of salespeople who believe that you are wrong. THEY'VE got the worst territory and YOU'VE got the best and they'd like the opportunity to work your territory in the same way that you feel that you might like to work theirs.

TIP 49
Recognize Your Own Value

When you're offered another job that pays more, one of life's truisms applies. You'll either get paid more than you're worth for a shorter period of time or get paid what you're worth for as long as you're worth it.

Understand and Recognize Your Own Value

Many people find another job for the right reason. That reason is that they are unable to be totally loyal to their employer. This usually leads to them insulting their management, their strategies or their support teams, which is neither healthy for the individual nor the employer.

TIP 50 — Do More than You are Paid to Do

How would you like to become too valuable to keep your present job at your present pay?

The secret was discovered years ago by someone who searched, researched and interviewed everybody who is anybody. He found the answer, the common denominator of successful people through history.

Do more than you are paid to do. Give better service than you are paid to give.

If you follow this advice, I can assure you that you will become too valuable to keep in your present job at your present pay.

In every company, there are a group of people who are permanent members of this club. They come wandering into the building at about nine o'clock and immediately head for the coffee area. Here they sit at large round tables and lie to each other. Finally, at about nine-thirty they get up and go to work.

Now the common factor that can be applied to all these people is that they are all poor performers. So don't be associated with them and don't join the coffee club.

TIP 52

It's curious, but the same people who are members of the coffee club are usually members of this club.

They leave the office at twelve-thirty or five-thirty (or earlier) and head for the pub or wine bar. Here they tell more lies about why they lost the order.

They don't realize that they cannot lose anything that they've never had.

Again, the common factor is that they are all poor performers.

Do you find that there is simply insufficient time during the day to accomplish all that you set out to do?

It's been said that 'time is life and that it's irreversible and irreplaceable. To waste your time is to waste your life. But to master your time is to master your life'.

So, how would you like to do more in less time?

Take a day out of your life to get yourself organized for the rest of your life.

Sign up on a professional Time Management course. These courses teach you to use your brain. They teach you to use your thinking power more effectively and you'll learn to put more thinking into what you do and not take the thinking out. You will become an 'effectiveness' expert.

A key principle of Time Management is DO IT NOW. What is it that you're doing right now (apart from reading this book), or earning the respect of your customers, that is more important than becoming organized for the rest of your life?

Remember, we all have the same amount of time during the day. The biggest difference between you and your competitor is how you use it.

If, by being more effective in the use of your

time, you could find a further 15 minutes a day, that would mean an extra week a year!

TIP *54* *Learn to Communicate*

What does 'to communicate' mean?

Communication is any means of contact between two or more people, out of which impressions are made and attitudes are created.

'By Communications, I mean the simple process of getting information known by one person to the attention of other people who should have this information . . .'

T. J. Watson, Jnr

Communications is at the core of all organized human activity. Literally, nothing happens until we communicate. A large number of problems can be traced to communications failure – that failure of your prospect to understand your proposal, for example. People tend to fear what they don't know or understand.

So, this applies to YOU!

The basic requirements for effective communication with your prospects and customers are:

- Honesty of purpose
- Common interest
- Mutual respect
- Desire to understand
- Message that helps
- Meaning that is clear

The secret of communication is creating an atmosphere where people exchange ideas and proposals informally and freely. In your case, this means you need to exchange ideas freely with your prospects and your customers. The job of communicating is not finished until there is *understanding*, *acceptance* and *resulting action*.

Remember that the rewards of successful two-way communications are great, but the pathway is often difficult:

● *Clarify* your ideas before communicating. Make them concise. Analyze your proposals before you discuss them.
● Consider the wider context. Think about timing, cultural differences and past experience before you make contact.
● Be aware of '*overtones*'. Think about the tone of voice, choice of language, expression and apparent receptiveness.
● Communicate for *tomorrow* as well as *today*. Be consistent with your prospect's and customer's long-range interests and goals.
● Seek not only to be *understood*, but to *understand*. Listen with that inner ear if you are to know the inner man.

Don't forget that there is a positive relationship between the quality of communication and results. The personal regard that your prospects have for you will affect the reception and acceptance of your proposals.

TIP 55

Assess Your Current
Presentation Skills

How well do your presentation skills stand up to scrutiny. Assess them against the headings of *PREPARATION and ORGANIZATION?*

PREPARATION

- *Have I a purpose*? By specifying your objective, you are determining whether you are there to persuade, to educate, to convince, to justify, to reach a decision or to take action, and the points covered in your presentation should directly support both your customer's expectations and objectives as well as your own.
- *Have I understood my audience*? This will bring focus to your presentation. Who are the decision-makers? How familiar with the topic are they? How interested are they? What is at stake and what is their attitude?
- *Have I an outline*? Have you identified the key topics of your presentation? Have you arranged them in a logical order so that they state your purpose simply and concisely?

ORGANIZATION

- *Have I an opening*? Will you introduce your topics and build credibility by reviewing the events that have led to your presentation?

Will you clearly state your objectives, including the level of commitment that you expect?

● *Have I an agenda*? Do you intend to review the topics that will be covered during the presentation?

● *Have I a 'body' to my presentation*?

  • How will you OVERVIEW the topics? Will you briefly and concisely discuss your customer's goals and objectives in the light of your customer's mission?

  • How will you REVIEW your customer's requirements? You should have identified and agreed these requirements with your customer on previous discussions.

  • How will you DISCUSS your solution? Will you give a general overview of your solution, highlighting the features and advantages? Will you clearly relate them to your customer's agreed needs?

  • How will you cover BENEFITS? Will you translate the advantages into actual customer benefits? Will these be a monetary amount that justifies the cost of your proposals? Do you believe that your customer will buy your solution based upon your presented benefits?

  • How will you CLOSE? How will you summarize the topics discussed? How will you outline your action plan, what you want your audience to do based on what you have just told them?

Attend that course on presentation skills and stand out from the crowd.

TIP 56 *Be Self-Critical*

Every time you fail to meet your call objectives, ask yourself, 'Why?' And if you can't arrive at an answer, ask your **CUSTOMER** 'Why?'

'Dear Mr Johnston, our meeting today was unsuccessful. We established an agreed need but we could not agree that my company should deliver the solution. Where did I go wrong?'

The answer will represent an objection and an objection is better than a 'No'!

That objection could relate to your technique, your personal skills, such as credibility, manner, rapport and sensitivity, or your professionalism, including your lack of product or service knowledge.

And you might just get back in.

TIP 57 *Be Enthusiastic*

The prime role of any salesperson is to persuade other people to take a course of action that we would like them to take.

The greatest principle of human persuasion that exists today can be summed up as follows:

'People are persuaded more by the depth of your conviction than by the height of your logic. More by your enthusiasm than by any proof that you can offer.'

People buy from enthusiastic people rather than tired and bored people.

If you were to ask Managing Directors of any consequence to give you the secret of success, they would come up with words like ability and energy. But they would also add that the real ingredient is enthusiasm and excitement.

Enthusiasm is one of the rarest qualities, yet it is the most contagious and even helps you to overcome fear.

There's only one rule. To became enthusiastic, act enthusiastically. And if you do that, you're winning before you even enter the battleground.

TIP *58* *A Reminder*

Is what you are doing right now contributing to your reaching your objectives? If not, why are you doing it?

If you have unplanned days, unqualified prospects, a haphazard timetable and travel schedule, an unused telephone, a long lunch hour with several drinks, are inefficient in your paperwork and take a short day, then you will never achieve any objectives of consequence.

Learn to plan, organize, control and measure your territory. These are the four fundamentals of territory management and you should set yourself objectives in each of them.

Think hard about the people who report to you.

This may seem pretty obvious, but it's only those sales managers who can positively answer the simple test below who can really call themselves sales managers.

- Do you have a specific, achievable and agreed career plan in place for each reporting salesperson?
- Are you fully aware of their individual abilities?
- Have you recognized their achievements?
- Do you have a training path that will improve their work and advance their careers?
- Do they have agreed job objectives?
- Do these agreed job objectives effectively use their range of capabilities?
- Have you actively worked with them to help them to achieve their objectives?
- Do they fully understand the factors that determine their salaries?
- Are you consistent in your personal interpretation of your company policies, practices and conditions?

TIP 60 What You Should Do Now

What can you do as a result of reading this book?

First, absolutely nothing. And if you do nothing, then buying this book will have been a total waste of money.

Second, you could decide to do something. You could say, 'Some of these ideas make sense and I've been reminded of some of the basic techniques that, today, I just don't use. Over the next few months I'll remember to incorporate these ideas into my selling activity.'

If you do that, you will also fail.

Third, you would take a more positive route. You could take a group of closely related Tips and give them a month's strict attention. Don't worry about the other Tips for this month. Concentrate on the ones that you have chosen.

If you concentrate like this, you'll gain confidence and become a truly great salesperson.

And in becoming so, you'll learn that you have been able to use some sixty small, unexceptional – though creative – ideas to such a level of effectiveness that the whole becomes an outstandingly good sale.

And if all else fails, there is another way. The Managing Director called in the Sales Manager for Southern Region and told him, 'I've decided to promote you to Chief Sales Director for the

UK and Europe, to give you a twenty thousand pound pay rise and also a piece of the equity. Young man, what do you say to that?'

'Thanks a lot, Dad!'

PART SIX

TO CLOSE

AIDE-MEMOIRE I

Closing Phrases

- I'm confident.

- I'm convinced.

- I believe.

- Let's do it.

- Let's go ahead.

- Let's get started.

- I recommend we do it.

- I would like to have your decision.

- Tell me where we stand. Let's go ahead.

- I need your approval to go ahead with this order.

- I would like your approval now to proceed.

- I would like your decision today.

- I'm going to ask for your commitment/support.

- In order to confirm a delivery date, I need you to okay this order.

- There is no real reason then as to why we should not proceed immediately with the order and implementation.

AIDE-MEMOIRE II

Tips for the Close

● Ask for the Order!

● Practice, practice, practice.

● Rehearse, rehearse, rehearse.

● Think of different ways of asking for the order.

● Make your own breaks.

● Sell what the customer wants to buy, not what you want to sell.

● Paint a picture.

● Accentuate the positive and the benefits.

● Be imaginative.

● Be creative.

● Concentrate on the solution.

● Sell what it does, not what it is.

● Don't be afraid of price.

● Anticipate objections in advance.

● Put yourself in your prospect's shoes – think like a buyer.

● Remember that each prospect is different.

● Tell them what you are going to do and do it.